FIERCE GRACE
COLLECTIVE

BY CARRIE-ANNE MOSS

To the women who day after day after day say yes
to the love and connection they desire.
To the women who are tired of pretending and pushing
through, I dedicate this to you ::

—Carrie-Anne

Women need council.
We need community.
We need support.

We want to live from our hearts. And yet life happens
and we shut down, we protect, we close off.

What if our hearts stay open regardless?

This is fierce grace.

11 STEPS TO ACTIVATE
FIERCE SPIRIT

(one) Practice fierce gratitude ... for everything. (two) When needed, get on your knees and and ask for deep love and support from your guides, your god, your spirits, your ancestors, your soul. (three) Say what you mean; mean what you say. Keeps things less complicated. Keeps things emotionally clean and tidy. (four) Meditate, even if it is for 3 minutes a day. Sit still. Close your eyes and connect to yourself. (five) Move your body—dance, run, walk, yoga, self care. (six) Keep moving forward. (seven) Open your heart through singing, prayer, laughter, or a big cry. (eight) Create art daily. Simple is just fine. Write a poem, draw a picture, make a meal, set a table. (nine) Be very kind—especially to yourself. (ten) Don't judge. (eleven) When you feel like judging, see how that something you want to judge is actually something within you—and have compassion for yourself and the thing or the person you wanted to judge.

CARRIE-ANNE MOSS

The Fierce Grace Collective is a sacred place to get clear and to connect to your dreams.

Your voice = Your fire = Your life.

STEPPING IN

Let us be strong here and clear. Let's stop apologizing for who we are. Let's stop playing small. Stop complaining. Stop being polite, and step into our Fierce Grace. That part of ourselves that values our journey, that knows that perfectionism and pretending are bullshit. We know that to do the important work we are each here to do, we must start with letting go of self doubt. The self doubt that lingers in comparison and shame. Let's understand that we need to keep up. We need our vitality. We need to step into our power day after day after day. Mind clear. Body vital. Heart open. Spirit full up.

FIERCE GRACE COLLECTIVE

"Tuning in.
Tuning in allows us to adjust our frequency to the right 'channel' that
we need to be in in order to receive and in order to give. That's what we
are doing when we chant 'Ong Namo Guru Dev Namo.'"

— *Carrie-Anne Moss*

"Sadhana.
What is sadhana? It's a committed prayer. It is something which you
want to do, have to do, and which is being done by you ... Sadhana is
self-enrichment. it is not something which is done to please somebody
or gain something. Sadhana is a personal process in which you bring
out your best."

— *Yogi Bhajan*

About Meditation

Kundalini yoga and Kundalini meditation were brought to the west by Yogi Bhajan in the 1960's. It is for people who are dealing with the stresses of life. You don't have to leave your home or sit on a mountain top; Kundalini yoga is for anyone who wants the skills and the tools to cope successfully with the challenges of living in these times.

Kundalini yoga is not a religion; it is a sacred science. Often, the terms "Kundalini yoga" and "meditation" can be used interchangeably. In this book we refer to Kundalini Yoga as taught by Yogi Bhajan.

About Sadhana (Daily Practice)

A daily practice is like putting daily deposits in a spiritual bank account. Or if it's not a daily practice, maybe it's a weekly practice, or a bi-weekly practice. Either way, it's adding to your sum total in the account. Every moment you invest in yourself matters. My Sadhana gives me the ability to download and receive and to be open and receptive to information.

There are so many ways to meditate. I choose Kundalini because it works for me in a way that no other meditation has. The biggest gifts I have received from my Kundalini practice are self-love, self-acceptance and knowing the power of presence. Creating this space within gives me the clarity to create the life that I crave.

Tuning In

In the tradition of Kundalini, before we begin our meditation we "tune in." This means we chant the mantra ONG NAMO GURU DEV NAMO three times. When we chant this, we are tuning into the divine teacher within us and all of the great teachers who have come before us. We are centering ourselves in this sacred space. Then we are ready to begin our meditation.

Closing

To close our meditation practice in Kundalini yoga, we sing or say this blessing three times:

May the long time sun shine upon you
all love surround you
And the pure light within you
guide your way on.

First to someone who needs it, perhaps someone you are holding anger or resentment toward. The second time is to yourself, and the third is for the world we live in.

How to Tune In

In Kundalini Yoga,
we begin every meditation by *tuning in*.
To tune in, chant three times:

ONG NAMO GURU DEV NAMO

This means roughly:

*"I bow to the divine teacher within and all the divine
teachers who have come before me."*

For an extended tuning in,
we follow the first chant with the following chant:

AAD GURAY NAMEH
JUGAAD GURAY NAMEH
SAT GURAY NAMEH
SIRI GURU DAYVAY NAMEH

Which means roughly:

*"I bow to the primal wisdom
I bow to the wisdom true through the ages
I bow to the true wisdom
I bow to the great unseen wisdom."*

When we close a meditation, we sing:

MAY THE LONG TIME SUN SHINE UPON YOU
ALL LOVE SURROUND YOU
AND THE PURE LIGHT WITHIN YOU
GUIDE YOUR WAY HOME

FIVE SUTRAS OF THE AQUARIAN AGE

BY
YOGI BHAJAN

RECOGNIZE THAT THE OTHER PERSON IS YOU

THERE IS A WAY THROUGH EVERY BLOCK

WHEN THE TIME IS ON YOU, START, AND THE PRESSURE WILL BE OFF

UNDERSTAND THROUGH COMPASSION OR YOU WILL MISUNDERSTAND THE TIMES

VIBRATE THE COSMOS, AND THE COSMOS SHALL CLEAR THE PATH

New Moon

Waning Moon

Waxing Moon

Full Moon

About the Moon

The **New Moon** is viewed as the beginning of the cycle. It is when you can't see the moon in the sky at all. This phase is associated with new beginnings, planting seeds, and setting intentions.

The **Full Moon** is the fullest point of the moon cycle, when you can see the entire moon in the sky. It is associated with fertility and creativity and the feeling of wrapping things up or harvesting what was planted.

The **Waxing Moon** is when the moon is going from New to Full. Think growth, gathering, expansion.

The **Waning Moon** is when the moon is going from Full to New, so it's getting smaller and fading. Think letting go, freedom, compost, self-care.

Of course, all of these are just guides. As you tune in, you will notice your own themes and patterns and begin to create your own rituals. Always listen to yourself and your own body above all else.

Weekly Moon Power Guide

Monday	Tuesday	Wednesday
MOON DAY	MARS DAY	MERCURY DAY
HOME day	GOALS day	BUSINESS day A creativity day A writing day A WISDOM day
Peace Sleep Healing Mystery Reflection Receptive reaction	Fire Energy goals	Air Communication sort and gather info collect
Moon and the sign of Cancer	Mars and Aries	Mercury and by signs of Virgo and Gemini
Frankincense, Jasmine	Pine, Garlic, Ginger	Peppermint, Lavender, Dandelion tea

Thursday JUPITER DAY	Friday VENUS DAY	Saturday SATURN DAY	Sunday SUN DAY
ASSIMILATION day	LOVE day	WISDOM DAY	SOUL day
Fire Abundance Growth Prosperity Success	Earth and Water Pleasure Happiness Wealth good fortune Arts BEAUTY female sexuality Friendship Music scent	Building Banks Knowledge Sacred Music	Air Creativity Joy Friendship Vitality Healing Leadership LIFEFORCE giver of life WHO ARE YOU AT THE CORE?
Jupiter and the sign of Sagittarius	Venus and the signs of Taurus and Libra	Saturn and by the sign of Capricorn	sun and by the sign of Leo
Cinnamon, Sage, Nutmeg	Rose Geranium, Magnolia	Patchouli, Cypress	Cedar

New Moon in Capricorn: December 26
Waxing phase: December 27, 2019-January 9, 2020
Full Moon in Cancer: January 10
Waning: January 11-January 23
New Moon in Aquarius: January 24

Notes to greet the new year/say goodbye to the old:

2019 was a wild, hard and
wonderful year.

leaving behind: lonliness, lostness,
overwhelm, isolation. Wasting time,
not doing what I want.

I say goodbye to not living
the life I want.

I say goodbye to Spiraling

I say goodbye to being overreactive

I say goodbye to being so in my head

I say goodbye to claiming sickness

I say goodbye to blocking Abundance

I say good by to not loving Myself

or My body.

I say goodbye to being stuck

I say goodbye to unhealthy patterns

I release old blocks and habits

I say goodby to lonliness and staying small

2019 was a wild, hard and
wonderful year.

leaving behind; loneliness, lostness,
not doing what I want

I say goodbye to not living
the life I want
I say goodbye to Spiraling
I say goodbye to being overreactive
I say goodbye to being so in my head
I say goodbye to claiming Sickness
I say goodbye to being Stuck
I say goodbye to loneliness and staying small

ROOTING

IN

Rooting In

New Moon in Aquarius
January 24

Full Moon in Leo
February 9

Gesture to live in:
I am not my feelings, but they are indicators and
secret messages of what I need.

Question:
If I were deeply rooted, who would I be?

Keywords:
Altar
Grounding
Practice
Foundation

Rooting In

To ground,
To be steady,
To feel supported,
To find strength from within.
To feel and be supported so that when I get triggered
by my stuff, my foundation holds me up.
It keeps me steady.
My foundation reminds me of who I am.
I remember who I am.
I am not my feelings.
My feelings are the canary in the coal mine—the
 ashing light in my car that reminds me I need to
refuel.
The blow-up in the kitchen is not about the thing
I'm screaming about, but about the tears underneath
it.

I am not my feelings,
but they are indicators, secret messages, reminders
of what I need.
They are the way through the block.
They are showing me where the block is.
Perhaps it's loneliness.
Perhaps I'm hungry.
Perhaps I need to weed out some extra weight that is
holding me down.
With a strong foundation, I can explore what's up
without falling apart so badly that I can't get up.

When my foundation is strong and true,
I can weather the storms.
I can keep on keeping up.
I can create,

I can love,
I can be clear,
I can be true to what I believe,
I can be kind.

I am not calm and stoic all the time
(of course I'm not)
I am, however, able to catch myself when I get hooked
and find a way to rise above.

My practice,
My foundation
Gives me this.

This is freedom for me::
In the quiet of the morning, I sit in the space of my
soul and I connect to my inner wisdom and the great
wisdom that is there for me.

It's there for you, too.
We just need to get quiet enough to hear it,
Even in this noisy world that tells us all day long
that there is more to want and more to be.
It's a world that doesn't truly value the feminine, and
so we must teach ourselves to value it. And then we
must pass that value on through example and inspiration
and expression.

When I sit in the quiet and start my day with
reverence,
I greatly shift the experience of my life.
From this shift

Anything is possible....

Foundation ::
Our practice::
Start here and be gentle with yourself.
Watch your life take shape.
Stuff will come up.
Times will challenge us.
A strong foundation and practice is the gateway to
freedom,
And it makes our roots
Grow deep.

Waxing Moon Phase: January 24-February 8. Full Moon February 9.

When we are rooted in ourselves, we are grounded and able to take care of our basic needs and feel comfortable in our bodies. When we are unbalanced at the root we can be fearful and insecure and life feels like a burden. We may feel we don't belong anywhere. Our constitution is weak. We have limited physical and mental strength.

Altars and meditation are two primary tools that help me feel rooted. But these are not the only tools. Breathing, slowing down, drinking tea, taking a bath, these are all things that ground me. Another thing that helps me is community. Women need other women. We need to confide in each other, laugh with each other, reflect with each other, gather, and connect.

You are not alone.

"Let your rituals hold you up, even when they feel routine or mundane. These are the times when your rituals are doing what they do best: gluing it all together with grace."

—Carrie-Anne Moss

Journal

02·10·19

This shift is big. I can feel it. I feel
both pushed and held by it. Understood
and at the same time blurred out.
 I feel tired, intense and grounded.

simultaneously fearful and full of love
and courage. Supported and alone.

The thing I want to feel
Most is clear and free.
Clear on my own tuition - when to
live, how to parent / homeschool / eat,
where to find my community, heal, baby,
 how to find my magic, know my soul,
rekindle.
and freedom - from generational
blocks, bonds, cycles. free from this
ground hogs day feeling. Free in my body,
                                    free in my
                                    mind, free

in my life, free in my days, free in my
motherhood, free in my magic, free in me.

Clarity & Freedom.

I long to be grounded in my own
intuition. to see. to know. to feel and
understand.

I long to be supported, wanted, cared
for and loved

I long for freedom and joy in my days.

I long for magic, ritual, rhythem, ease,
flow, to remember and be empowered.

I long for abundance, radiance, prosperity,
affluence, ease, flow, vitality, health, energy,
confidence

I long for a clear head, good concentration,
attention span, knowing, truth

I long to be the clearst, fullest, wholest,
truest, most radiant, abundant, beautiful
version of me.
        to love myself
        and my life

Clarity & freedom.

I long to be guided by my own
intuition. To see, to know, to feel what
understand.

I long to be supported, wanted, loved

I long for freedom and joy in my days.

How, to remember and be empowered.

I long for a clear head, good concentration,

Waning Moon Phase: February 9–February 22. New Moon February 23.

Each day, notice what you love and what you don't. Listen to yourself if you're groaning about a commitment or obligation. Noticing is powerful and being at peace with what you notice is even more powerful. Don't resist your true feelings. If you do, the feeling will keep returning until you look at it. There is great power in setting intentions, in creating a disciplined meditation practice, and in creating the life you desire. I honor you and your dedication and I encourage you to nourish yourself through not only what you eat and do, but through what you think and decide.

Journal

Journal

DANCE OF THE POET

Dance of the Poet

New Moon in Pisces
February 23

Full Moon in Virgo
March 9

Gesture to live in:
I create the life I want with the choices I make
and the actions I take.

Question:
Who do I want to be?

Keywords:
Dance
Create
Listen
Do

Dance of the Poet

Creativity is the gateway to the life I want.
I am an artist.
I didn't always feel like one, but when I embraced
that yes I am an artist, my life started to shift.
We are all artists.
We are always creating.
We are always giving birth
To ideas,
To new ways,
To gardens (metaphorically and physically).
I am an artist when I creatively tend to my loves.
I am an artist when I boil water for tea.
I am an artist when I look my kid in the eyes and
tell him how I feel and ask what's up with him.
My husband reads a lot of deep spiritual text. He's
a hardy New England soul and not fluffy in any way.
One afternoon he shared with me and our little girl
and our beloved Celeste who helps us at home about a
part of meditation that he was exploring. We all sat
on the floor in the kitchen and he led us through
the mediation. We chanted, we whispered, then we
mentally chanted and then he said, "now listen for
the sound."

Wow.
Listen for the sound::
What is the sound of your life?
Throughout your day, take the time to listen to your
life.
You are the writer, the director, the producer, and
the star of your life.
You create the life you want by the choices you make
and the actions you take.
Life will challenge us.
Be an artist.
Be creative, and simple things will feel divine.
Be a poet and a dancer and bring all of your body,
your soul, and your being to your glorious life one
breath at at time....
You are the poet. You get to write it.

Waxing Moon Phase: February 24-March 8. Full Moon March 9.

As a woman you are a creator. You are the poet in a constant dance with life. With every movement, word, thought, and soul-song you are weaving together the ordinary beauty that is life. To embrace the body of the poet is to simply choose to see the magic in your ordinary day. It is to breathe, notice, and revere. It is to bring awareness to your own song, the song you sing each moment, the vibration you carry with you everywhere you go.

Bringing awareness to your own uniqueness involves a simultaneous awareness of your inner self and your outer self. It involves taking responsibility for who you are in each moment.

For me, this is a recurring theme. I think "it is not *what* do I want to be, but *who* I want to be."

Who do you want to be? How can you become this? Are you already who you want to be? Our circumstances do not define us. Your job does not define you. What is in your heart defines you, and the actions that you take each day define your life.

"Softness is when I surrender to what is and at the same time keep moving forward. It is when I surrender to what is without giving up. And if I need to let it go, I will."

—Carrie-Anne Moss

Journal

Journal

Waning Moon Phase: March 10-23. New Moon March 24.

Through discipline, we soften our load. Discipline makes things easier. This seems counterintuitive at first because discipline may seem like a struggle or like it's too rigid. But true discipline is marvelous mastery of the self. It means you know your NO and your YES and you know when to use them. It means you have boundaries for yourself, which means everything else flows through you with ease and grace.

What does discipline mean to you? What is your relationship with it? Write it down.

I have read a lot about discipline. I've read about it in regards to my meditation practice, in regards to parenting, and in regards to acting. Discipline manifests in many ways. I think the problem is that discipline gets confused for *rules*. Rules are external while discipline is internal.

Discipline comes from your deep center.

Journal

Journal

TEMPLE
BODY

Temple Body

New Moon in Aries
March 24

Full Moon in Libra
April 8

Gesture to live in:
Strong center, soft heart.

Question:
How do I feel?

Keywords:
Strength
Connection
Integrity
Passion

Temple Body

Dear Me,
I honor you for always wanting to grow and stretch.
I honor you for the places that are hard to trust.
I honor that there are times you feel afraid
and you hold on too tightly.

Dear Me,
I see your perfection and the way you love others so much.
I see the way you care about people you don't even know.
I see the way you feel when there is unkindness in the air.

Dear Me,
I care about you.
I care about the way you feel.
I care about the way you move.

Dear Me,
I promise to love you no matter what.
I promise to be there for you always.
I promise to never abandon you.

Dear Me,
I wish for you to feel all that you are.
I wish that your life expands
and that you feel the magic all around you.
I wish that your creativity lights the way
for you and others.

Dear Me,
I love you.

Waxing Moon Phase: March 25-April 7. Full Moon April 8.

In Kundalini yoga, we refer to the "Navel Center" which is a point on your body about 2-3" below your belly button. When this place is strong, you have the ability to stay centered within yourself. An activated navel gives you stamina and motivation to commit to do what you need to do and to take action when you need to. It helps you say what you mean. When the navel center is weak or out of balance, you may feel unmotivated and unclear.

The navel is your center. It is an anchor point, a pivot point from which all action is birthed. When the anchor is strong, you feel free. Having a strong center comes from having a strong practice of attention to the self and to intuition. This is why I so very much recommend meditation for this particular aspect. It helps strengthen and attune that which is otherwise hard to understand.

Being strong in your center is a way that you can be present in your life. It is how you can set boundaries with grace. In this way, you begin to create a life you truly love. This benefits you, your family, and the people around you. When you are strong, you allow others to be strong. When you are authentic, you give space for others to be authentic.

"Become acutely aware of your body and the messages it sends. What is unfurling in you right now?"

—Carrie-Anne Moss

Journal

Journal

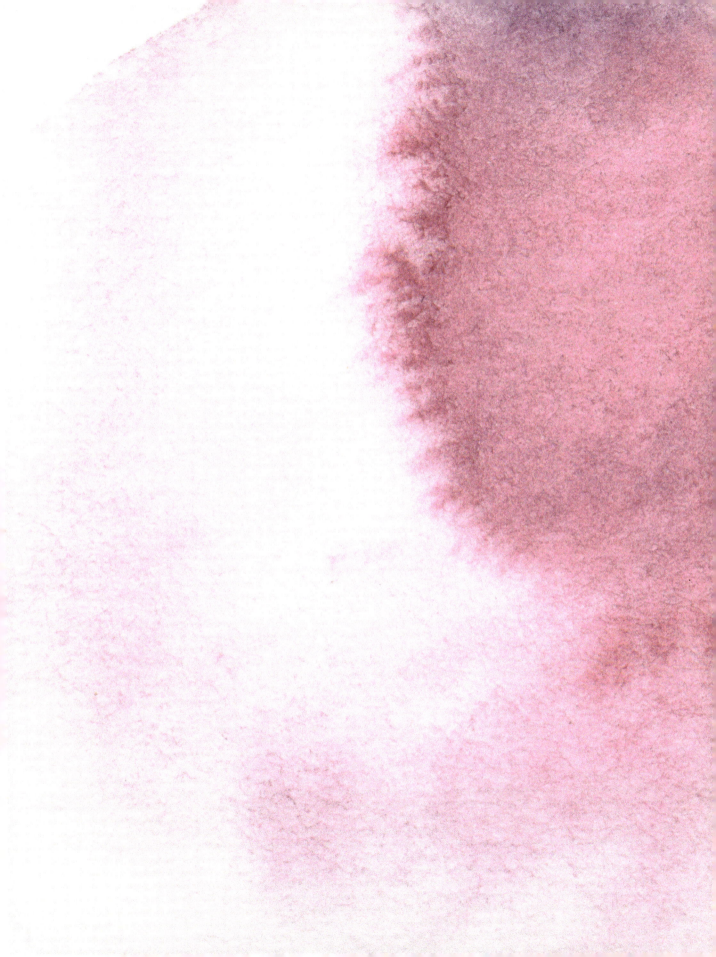

Waning Moon Phase: April 9-22. New Moon April 23.

The body is a map. It is a map to your intuition, to your heart, and to your life. Anything that comes up, you can find it in the body. Many stresses manifest as illness, and joy can manifest as glowing skin or supreme health. The two are always intertwined.

We are taught to ignore our feelings and to let logic rule our choices. Because of this, we are quick to dismiss what rises in the belly because it lacks tangible proof. But those first feelings, that gut instinct, is not to be ignored.

Look back over the years that have made up your life and count all of the moments where you went against your instinct. What was the result? And what about all of the times when you went by feeling, even when it didn't make sense to you or anyone else?

When we listen to our bodies and feel strong in our center, we emanate a subtle strength that makes us, and those around us, feel safe. And when we feel strong and safe, we move and live differently. We don't think, "*How do I look?*" But instead we think, "*How do I feel?*"

Journal

Journal

Beauty Emerge

New Moon in Taurus
April 23

Full Moon in Scorpio
May 7

Gesture to live in:
Holding my heart with reverence is an exquisite
act of self-care.

Question:
How can I be of service?

Keywords:
Gratitude
Service
Challenge
Opportunity

Beauty Emerge

Your heart,
your beautiful heart.
Keeping your heart open even when the world is aching
is a radical act.
We do it because it is the work.
It is the portal into the world we desire.

It starts with gratitude::
Feeling grateful,
Being grateful..
Living in gratitude.

Building my life on gratitude.
Building the house that I live in, painting the
walls, finishing the roof with gratitude.
Thank you for this door.
Thank you for this home.
Thank you for this opportunity, and this one and
this one.
Thank you for the challenge that breaks me wide open.
Thank you for the food and the hands that prepared
the food.
Thank you for these hands and this breath and this
one and this one too...
Thank you, thank you, thank you.

When I was younger and only had myself to think
about, my dear friend and mentor Kathleen would
suggest I do things that put me in service whenever
I was struggling with an issue. I understand now
what she was teaching me.
How can I serve?
How can I live in service?

Being of service and living in gratitude are the
gateways to my peace of mind, and my peace of mind
is my wealth.
Holding my heart with reverence and care are
exquisite acts of self care.

My beauty is not for sale.
My heart is a vessel of love.
My beauty is radiant and lives within me.
my heart is supporting me and holding me up.
My beauty is effervescent and a reflection of my soul.
My heart is strong and steady.

Beauty Emerge....

Waxing Moon Phase: April 24-May 6. Full Moon May 7.

Beauty Emerge is about intimacy with our lives and with
who we are. Living within our lives starts by sharing
our true authentic selves with others. Sharing our true
selves is scary and it takes courage. It takes knowing
when to say no and when to say yes. Stop watching from
the sidelines, afraid to share your gifts or yourself
with the world. It's time to share who you are.

Compassion and courage are both heart-centered. I
believe it takes courage to have compassion. It is easy
to hide behind judgment and blame, but when we take a
moment to see if we can reach for compassion instead,
everything changes. Not just for us, but for the people
around us as well.

In a situation where you feel confused or frustrated,
take a moment to consider: what is the most generous
thing I can do right now? What can I give? Who needs the
most love in this situation?

As you move through this month, be aware of your heart
center. Stretch it daily. Open up to the sun, the sky,
your loved ones. Be open. As you adjust your body and
your surroundings, you also adjust your inner self and
begin to expand outward into the space you have created.

Let your beauty emerge.

"In everything, there is elegance and grace. It is up to us to find these things and to embody them. When we act in compassion, we begin to change ourselves and the world around us, because acting in compassion is acting in love."

—Carrie-Anne Moss

Journal

Journal

Waning Moon Phase: May 8-21. New Moon May 22.

There is power in action. We don't need to simmer in the anticipation or fear of change or sharing. When we feel pressured about something, the release valve lies in taking action to catalyze a shift. Then we move out of the pressure zone. If we stay under pressure, it creates stress and then it is harder to be graceful. It's easy to trap ourselves in a state of pressure.

Remember, when the pressure is on, get started, and the pressure comes off. Start with small steps. Make a list and start with the first tiny thing. It's a process of clearing away cobwebs, or cleaning windows. Have you ever been driving and you don't notice how dirty the windshield is, and then once you clean it, you can't believe how different it is? Apply this to your life. Where is there tension, fear or pressure? It's time to scrub it out so that you can see clearly and so the sun can shine in.

Just as you clean the windows of your home and your car, remember to clean the windows of your body and spirit. But how do you do this? You ask. Well, sometimes when I want to work on the inside, I start with the outside. Perhaps it is time to literally clean your windows. Have they been cleaned recently? Which are the ones you look out of the most? Start there. Look into the corners of your home: are they dusty? Look at the places you use the most. Are they messy and stagnant? Clean them up.

By honoring our spaces in these ways, we honor ourselves.

Journal

Journal

ALCHEMY
SPEAK

Alchemy Speak

New Moon in Gemini
May 22

Full Moon in Sagittarius
June 5

Gesture to live in:
I speak my life into being.

Question:
How do I communicate with the world?

Keywords:
Communication
Truth
Knowing
Saying

Alchemy Speak

I am speaking my life into being.
I am speaking me into being.

That story I love to tell, the one about how
disappointed I was. That story I tell so that I can
relate and connect and bond.
That story that sends me into panic that is living
only inside my mind...

I don't want or need to tell old stories that are
habitual.
I will speak my beautiful, glorious life into action
by speaking it out loud.
By breathing it into being,
By imagining it
as so.

Yes, I have been through so much and I will not
pretend that I haven't.
I won't lie and say I'm rosy when I am having a
hard time,
BUT...

I will be more inclined to rewrite the story ... to
catch myself when I start to compare complain and
gossip.

I will see that wanting to tell that story again may
be a sign that I'm lonely and I need to find other
ways to connect.

I don't need to bond over hardships.
I can bond over hope and dreams and lifting up.
I will empower you to step into your greatness, your
beauty, and I will do the same for me.
The old habitual stories that no longer serve must
be let go through discipline and devotion.

If we want our lives to be a true reflection of our
souls,then we need to STOP playing small by repeating the
stories that don't serve us.

Share yourself with the world but pay attention to
the way you are speaking about yourself...
Be a good friend to yourself and treat yourself with
respect
through words and actions.

Speak your life into being.

Waxing Moon Phase: May 23-June 4. Full Moon June 5.

We create our reality with the words we speak. Knowing this, it's time to break our bad habits of negative dis-empowering language. This includes negative self-talk and negative gossip. This takes discipline. And oh, don't I know it! Bring the bad habits to the fire and let them go in order to create a new story.

Ask yourself, *what is my authentic voice? What do I want to say? What do I want people to hear?* When you go through the day complaining, ranting, or criticizing, you get back the energy you put out. Instead, go about your day complimenting, being generous, and lifting up others. You'll get the same in return.

How do you speak to people? To loved ones? To strangers? What assumptions do you make? Words can hurt. An unkind word is often sharper than a knife. Be aware of the communication tools you have and how you use them.

Communication is a gift. Centered in the throat chakra, communication connects to our health, clarity and confidence. When our throat center is open and strong, it functions as such. When it is weak, it results in shyness, trouble communicating clearly, insecurity, and even throat or voice problems. Much of this manifests as a fear of other people's opinions and judgment.

Stay rooted in your own confidence and choices. Be mindful of complaining and gossip. These words do no good for you or the world around you.

"I speak kindly and clearly and truthfully. I am impeccable with my word."

"Singing clears out the throat chakra and removes obstacles of communication. Singing clears the pathways. Singing brings the light."

—Carrie-Anne Moss

Journal

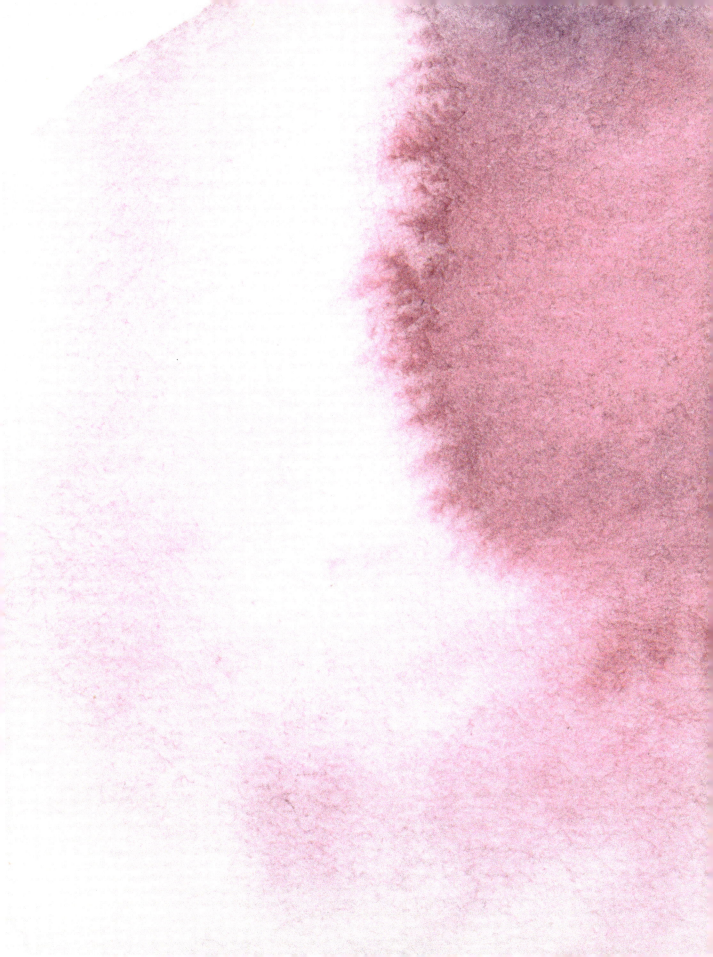

Journal

Waning Moon Phase: June 6-June 20. New Moon June 21.

Our lives are consuming and we forget our needs
altogether. In a day full of bits and pieces and driving
and dishes, our needs fall between the cracks.
Eventually we break down. It is our job to first be
aware of our needs. This takes commitment and some
moments of silence. Second, we must communicate these
needs, otherwise they simply will not be met. Not by us,
by our partners, by our children, or by our co-workers.

Do you need to be alone from 3-4 pm? Do you need to go
to bed earlier? Begin to shift things so that whatever
it is is possible. Ask yourself, *what do I need?*

Once you know what you need, then you can speak it. When
you don't know what you need, how can you expect another
person to know your needs? Write your needs down. Keep
track. Don't expect others to read your mind. This
always ends in disappointment.

Be crystal clear. Communicate exactly. "Can you please
rub my shoulders?" "Can you make me a tea please?"
Saying, "You never do anything for me" will not inspire
anyone to help you, so don't let it get to that point.
Even saying, "I need your support" is not clear enough.
Say what kind of support you need. Sometimes we just
need to be held, sometimes we need help making
decisions, sometimes we need people to come help us pack
boxes and move into a new house. Sometimes we are sick
and need someone to come over and help with our children
or with dinner.

Be as specific as you can, and everyone benefits.

Journal

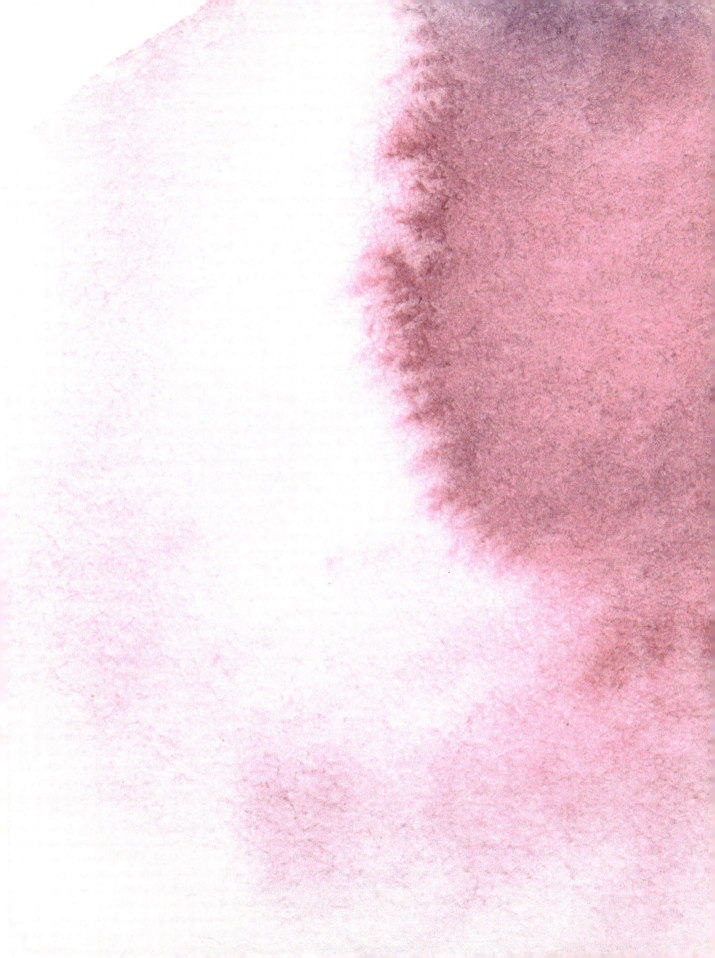

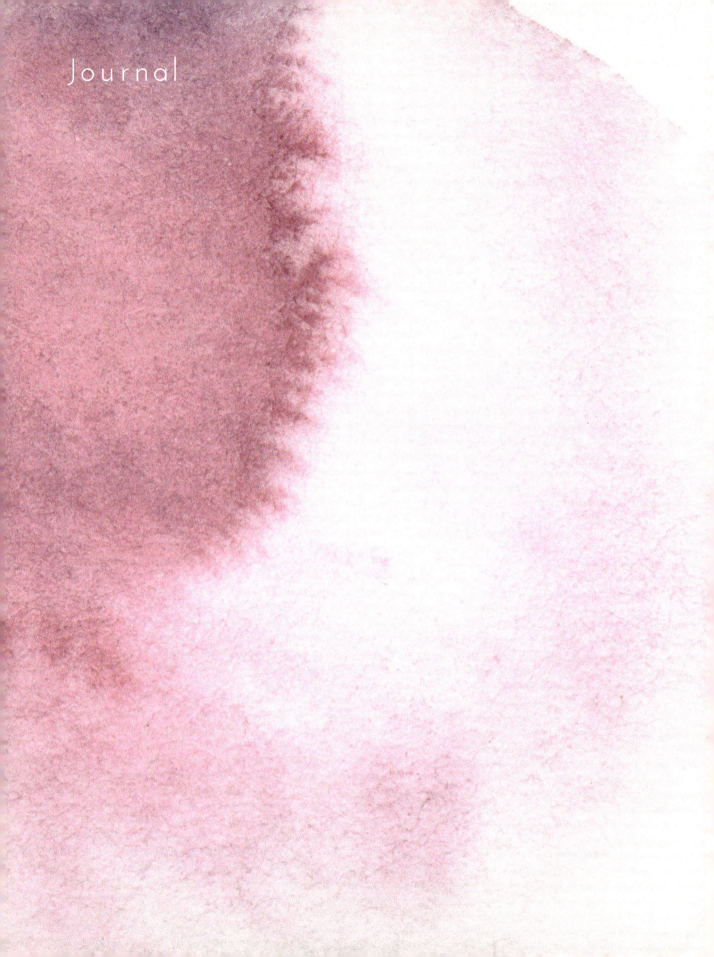

Journal

IN HER LIGHT

In Her Light

New Moon in Cancer
June 21

Full Moon in Capricorn
July 5

Gesture to live in:
I know what it feels like to know.

Question:
What does my intuition feel like?

Keywords:
Intuition
Relaxation
Listening
Laughter

In Her Light

Dear intuition, the part of me that knows,
I bow to you.
I am sorry that I haven't always trusted you.
I am sorry that so many of my sisters have been
stripped of their connection to you.
I stand here today to welcome you,
to witness you, and to receive your wisdom.
My intuition is blessed.
My intuition is the sound of my highest.
My intuition lives within me and surrounds me with
protection and projection of soul.

Subtle and sometimes striking—
I hear you,
I know you,
I honor you,
I appreciate you.
Grounded am I
So that I can hear you.
Steady am I
so that I can feel you.
Open am I
so that bravely I can live in you
In my light I live
In my light I love
In my light I share
In my light I am enough.

Waxing Moon Phase: June 22-July 4. Full Moon July 5.

Creating rhythm to cultivate ease and relaxation in your full, busy life will naturally make you more intuitive and help you connect to your higher self. Creating rhythm takes effort at first, but after that it becomes easier as you relax into it. Tune into what your body really wants, and begin basing your rhythm off of that.

Create rituals that foster rhythm.

Rituals can be easy and simple. Turn toward the subtle, the quiet, and the mundane. There's ritual in your life already: the tea in the morning, the way you get dressed, the face wash, then the serum, then the moisturizer, in that order, every time. Perhaps the way your child wakes you up, or the way you text your honey before bed every night. Look at these small rhythms. These are your rituals. Which ones fill you up the most?

When was the last time you relaxed? Sometimes the greatest act of rebellion is going into our bedrooms and laying down in the middle of the afternoon.

"As we create nurturing rituals, our rituals support us with ease and grace. Without even thinking, we flow through our rhythms like the sun moves through the sky."

—Carrie-Anne Moss

Journal

Journal

Waning Moon Phase: July 6-19. New Moon July 20.

An essential part of intuition is ownership. No one owns your intuition but you. It is one of the things in life that is entirely, uniquely yours. There is no measuring stick for it, no where to crosscheck its viability or performance. Every single aspect of it comes from within. You cannot compare your inner truth to any outer truths and hope for success, because it's not there.

The only measure of your intuition is in your heart and in your belly. Owning your intuition makes it more powerful because you are giving it permission to thrive. It also makes it stronger because it knows that you are listening. The reciprocal relationship you have with it will continue to strengthen exponentially.

Ownership is tied to freedom. Freedom means you can spread your wings, feel your heart, and sing to the world if you want. It also means you can carry it truth quietly in yourself, letting it lead the way.

Journal

Journal

WONDER WOMAN

Wonder Woman

New Moon in Cancer
July 20

Full Moon in Aquarius
August 3

Gesture to live in:
Like the moon, I change.

Question:
How do I relate to the moon?

Keywords:
Gather
Release
Allow
Feel

Wonder Woman

Like the moon, I change.
Oh sweet and sacred moon,
you give me everything I need to hold myself through
the tides of my life.
I anchor to you in gratitude and in absolute
surrender.
It has taken me my whole life to give you the credit
you deserve, and the gratitude you never expect.
If only my younger me had known the power of you.
I sigh in relief when I align with you.
I choose you over mainstream ways of telling time
and setting intentions.
You watch over me, you guide me, you support me, and
inspire me.
What can I do for you Beauty Moon?
How can I thank you?
I hear you clearly respond:
Be all that you are.
Be full like me.
Accept yourself.
Love yourself.
Shine brightly, and trust the times when you go
inward and need shelter.
Know that you, too, are like me... full of everything
you need to thrive.
Be steady, woman. You are held, you are seen, and
you are enough.

I wrote this song when I was 11 years old:
I was walking around the corner, and what do you think I saw?
I saw a star as bright as the sun.
I thought it would be rather fun
to be up in the air with that little star.
To be flying up above with that little star.
The very next day that little star was gone.
My eyes were filled with tears because there's no more fun.
To be up in the air with that little star to be flying up above with that little star.

May we look up to the sky and feel supported by the sky, the moon, the sun, and the stars.
May we remember our innocence in the magic of the sky.
May we have hope where we feel fear.
May we be held by the earth.
May we have faith when we feel hardened.
May we choose to live our lives with a connection to our souls.
May we remember who we are.
And who we are is...

Exquisite.

Waxing Moon Phase: July 20-August 2. Full Moon August 3.

The new moon is the point of total darkness, where there
is no moonlight in the sky. This darkness is an
opportunity for rebirth, regrowth, and for shedding. It
is when the vessel is empty so that it can be filled
again; it is when the dirt is rich and tilled so that
seeds can be planted.Every new moon brings with it a
particular feeling. It is up to you to find out what
these feelings are. Now I invite you to abandon any
preconceived notion you've ever had about the new moon
and tune in to you.

I have found so much relief in the moon. It's taught me
that sometimes I will be strong, sometimes I will be a
mess, sometimes I will be restless, and sometimes I will
be at peace. Knowing that these things cycle with the
moon has made me feel empowered and able to let go,
while also feeling more in control. As the moon waxes,
things begin to grow and take shape. Dreams materialize
and visions become clearer. A keyword for this phase is
gathering.

Gathering strength, gathering light, gathering shape,
gathering gravity. The moon is gathering right now as
she heads to fullness. What are you gathering? What is
gathering around you?

"Like the moon, I change. Like the moon, so do you."

Catherine Muse

Journal

Journal

Waning Moon Phase: August 4-18. New Moon August 19.

The waning moon cycle is like the sigh of relief after the full moon. The archetype associated with this phase is the Wise Woman, the woman who no longer cycles but has moved onto the esteemed realm of elders. During this phase, the moon is getting smaller. The fullness is receding into the dark. The moon is still there, as always, but she's partially hiding from the sun and choosing not to reflect so much light.

We all need times like this, where we choose not to shine, where we choose not to reflect or stand out or sing to the world. We need times where we retreat, rest, and withdraw into the quiet comfort of ourselves. We need to shed what doesn't serve us and what holds us back.

Just as each day has a sunset and each month has a waning moon, we as women have our own period of retreat, our own personal golden hour.

Journal

Journal

VENUS & GOLD

Venus & Gold

New Moon in Leo
August 19

Full Moon in Pisces
September 2

Gesture to live in:
I no longer need external validation.

Question:
Where does goddess show up in my life?

Keywords:
Possibility
Mystery
Divinity
Pleasure

Venus & Gold

Goddess::
Pleasure and beauty,
a single flower in a mason jar.
Coconut oil all over my body before a shower.
Washing my feet before bed.
Listening to music with lights low as I brush my
teeth.
My favorite essential oil on my pillow.
An old silk dress that's holding on by a thread, but
makes me feel gorgeous.

I choose you, Goddess
I see you all around me
I choose you by accepting myself and letting go of
limitation.

The Goddess is me.
She is you.

She is in the drink I made last night.
She is in the quiet of the night when I forget who I
am and then find myself all over again.

I am not afraid of getting lost anymore because I
know that whatever I will find will be truer than
before.
I don't need anything or anyone to validate me.
But if I listen carefully, the world I want is
whispering words of true encouragement into my ear.
(The world I do not want is telling me I'm not doing
it right).

I choose the world I want::
I choose me.

I choose.

I choose.

I choose.

Waxing Moon Phase: August 20-September 1. Full Moon September 2.

The Goddess doesn't look any certain way. She's not always wearing a flowy dress nor does she always have long locks of hair. Women who embody the true Goddess source show up in many ways. We associate Goddess energy with a certain way of looking or acting, but in truth the real Goddess energy shows up in women's ways of BEING. The Goddess knows no boundaries and she is not restricted by trends or styles. She simply IS.

The Goddess energy lives in you. This believing and knowing is available to all women. Remember to never compare your insides with someone else's outsides. Who/ what Goddess is for me will be different than who/what Goddess is for you. We look to our teachers for guidance, yet our own process and truth will always be different than the process and truth of even our most beloved teachers.

This is the call to courage. We must own our knowledge. We must own our power and intuition. We can look around us for inspiration, but the true embodiment only comes from ourselves.

"Goddess is not a person, a trend, or a look. She is many people, women, maiden mother and crone. She is an energy, she is kindness and fierce strength, she is saying NO even when others want us to say YES. She is wisdom and truth, that feeling in our gut when we know what is right. She is Mother Earth, the water and the trees, the oceans and rivers, the beds in which we plant our gardens."

—Carrie-Anne Moss

Journal

Journal

Waning Moon Phase: September 3-16. New Moon September 17.

There's divine wisdom within women. It is one of the things we all have equal access to in this life. Many of us have strayed from our divine wisdom: we don't trust ourselves We see other women doing things, and we think, "she knows better," or sometimes we judge the way she is doing it and think, "I know better."

What if we all just settled into ourselves for the answers, grace and wisdom that lives within us, and reached out to support, uplift and to listen? What if we leaned on the women who nourish us to listen to us and hold us up? What if we offered an arm to hold up the women we love?

Holy wow. This is the revolution, women.
We cannot be bought or sold.
We are power-full.

The divine mystery of woman and Goddess is revealed in many ways. Gathering and supporting one another is one of the ways in which this magic is unlocked and magnified.

We must gather.
We must support.
We must create.

Journal

Journal

HOLDING HOME

Holding Home

New Moon in Virgo
September 17

Full Moon in Aries
October 1

Gesture to live in:
Home is where my heart is.

Question:
How do I relax?

Keywords:
Simplicity
Home
Simmer
Rest

Holding Home

I am home.
I embrace home within me.
I am in my home.
I create home wherever I go.

::I am home::

I hold myself as sacred.
I create a home that reflects my inner world by:

• Creating a simple and sincere altar
• Keeping soothing sounds in my home
• Making simple and nourishing food
• Taking a bath (with essential oils and Epsom salts)as a sacred self-care ritual
• Reading books that inspire and uplift me
• Creating reminders throughout my house of the values that are important to me

Home is a place where others feel nourished. Home is a place where I feel nourished. My physical home and my body home are for me to feel nourished, not to impress others.

When we create cozy homes, we create a place where we can be our true selves, love to our whole capacity, and feel joy from the simplicity of a mug in our hands, food on the kitchen table, a rug on our floor.

Home is
Where the heart is.

Waxing Moon Phase: September 18-30. Full Moon October 1.

The more sacred and cozy my home feels, the more I can relax my nervous system so that it can be deeply nourished. How do you relax? This is so important. Rest is a vital nutrient in our lives and in our days. Rest isn't just something to do when you're exhausted, but something that should be done before you're at that point. I love to create my home and space so that it is restful by nature; so that it heals me and helps me breathe, open, and expand. When my home is restful, I can truly be myself and find my center. Making a home is simply an everyday exercise in these two things: deep love, and raising the vibration.

Home is about heart and connection and happiness, and about that space where we can feel safe to be ourselves and live our truth. It's about nourishing through food and through peaceful space. It's about creating joy by simply existing where we belong, and appreciating the view.

"My home is my oasis of healing and love. My kitchen serves as my church, and my wood table is the altar of my family."

—Cecilia-Anne Moss

Journal

Journal

Waning Moon Phase: October 2-15. New Moon October 16.

As women, we are hungry for connection and community. We long for gatherings of women and feelings of sisterhood. Nothing binds together a gathering, a circle, or a connection quite so much as sharing food. Throughout history, food has so often bound women and families together. When we create ritual from our food duties, it they become wholly nourishing for us. If we view food as a communion with ourselves and those we love, then we are well on our way to deep happiness.

Home is where we return to when we need to heal, when we are worn out, and when the weight of the world is too much to bear. There is so much nourishment in our homes. It's in our beds, in our cupboards of tea or medicine, in the fruit bowl on the counter. However we take care of our bodies and spirits, it all starts at home. And so much of it is held together by food. Our homes give us space to nourish ourselves. The board to cut on, the stove to simmer the soup, the oven where we bake, roast, and toast.

Home is where we feed our bodies, and in doing so, our hearts. And home is where, even unknowingly, we gather.

Journal

Journal

RADIANCE
AWAKEN

Radiance Awaken

New Moon in Libra
October 16

Full Moon in Taurus
October 31

Gesture to live in:
Comparison is a distraction.

Question:
What makes me feel strong and beautiful?

Keywords:
Radiant
Free
Transform
Forgive

Radiance Awaken

Dear Queen,

I see you in your strength and grace.
I see you move with poise and grit, with joy and
care.
I see you handling conflict with intellect and
intuition.

I feel you when you enter the room.
Your true beauty is your radiance pouring out of you
from within...

Acceptance of self is the portal into your radiance.
Looking like the standard idea of beauty is not real.
You are real.
You are radiant.
You are beautiful.

Waxing Moon Phase: October 17-30. Full Moon October 31.

Radiance comes from the inside, and as you tend to it you help it grow and shine. As you strengthen your heart center, beauty radiates more freely and easily. How do we waste our energy? By complaining, competing, and comparing. Instead of complaining, look instead to see what is working. Nurture what is good. Instead of comparing yourself to anyone else, connect to yourself and ask yourself what you need. Connect to your truth and your soul and let those things be soft, let them shine. Know that you can never know truly what someone else's life is like. Comparing is a distraction from living your own life to its fullest. If you need to, take a break from social media so that you are not tempted to compare. Watch and see what happens as you recalibrate.

"I create the space inside of me to nurture and tune into the deepest part of myself: my soul. When I carve out ten minutes to sit quietly to breathe, to stretch, and to bring myself back to the center of my being, my life works and it is easier to live in the radiance I crave."

—Carrie-Anne Moss

Journal

Journal

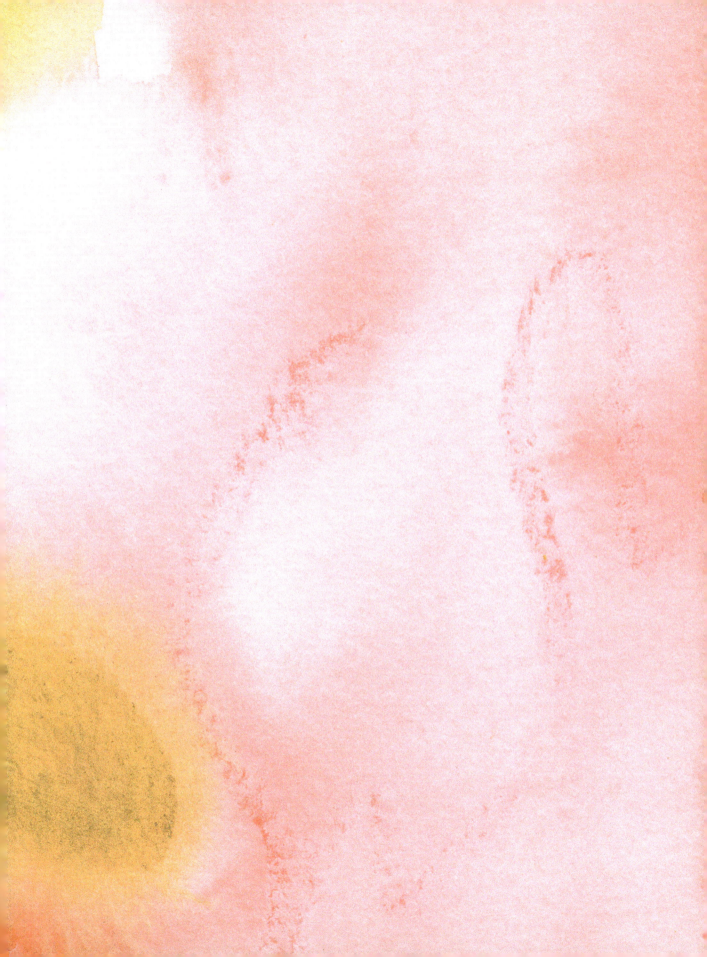

Waning Moon Phase: November 1-14. New Moon November 15.

As I sit at the altar of my soul, I know that being authentic is important to me. So I create the space inside to nurture and to tune in to the deepest part of myself: my soul. When I carve out time for my Sadhana, or even just 10 minutes to sit quietly and breathe, stretch, and bring myself back to the center of my being, my life works better. I find it easier to live in the radiance I crave. I find the ease to illuminate. In the space of this daily ritual I connect to myself, and when I do, these are some of the benefits I have witnessed in my life:

I forgive myself and others.
I have more patience.
I trust myself.
I love and cherish my body, respect it, and nourish it.
I feel more creative.
I sleep well.
I let go of what I think I know.
I transform my fear around aging and find the beauty in this time of my life.
I strengthen my core so that I can unleash my creativity and feel the power of my center.
I notice others who emanate strength and radiance.
I love myself with all my imperfections.
I dance and sing, tuning into my heart and my sensuality, raising my vibration.
I laugh.
I surrender it all.

A daily practice can fortify your radiance. Tune in and see what works for you.

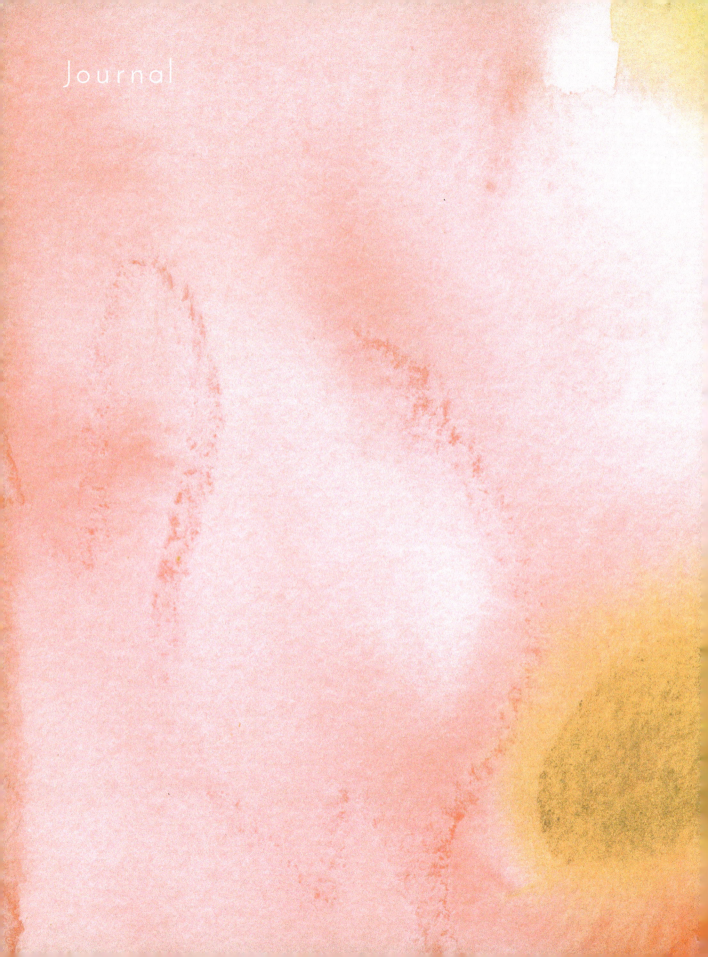

Journal

Journal

BY THE FIRE

By the Fire

New Moon in Scorpio
November 15

Full Moon in Gemini
November 30

Gesture to live in:
I create space for myself.

Question:
What do I have to offer?

Keywords:
Winter
Warmth
Remembrance
Renewal

By the Fire

I'm soft, you see.
I walk out the back door of my house in the dark of
the morning to gather wood for the fire.
I usually wear my slippers, but truth be told I can
do it barefoot because I live in California.
I'm soft and strong.
I'm privileged and grateful.
I remember my childhood, and growing up the way I
did means I never take my life for granted.
I appreciate the smallest of things because it makes
me happy.
I feel grateful for the walk outside in the morning,
it sets the tone for my life.
Listen for what the morning sounds like,
what the sky looks like.
Where is the moon?
Oh there she is...
hi...

I get to start again and again.
I light the re with simple reverence.
I feel like a Queen, but please don't take a picture,
because I most likely don't look like one in my
mismatched outfit and crazy hair (but I don't care).
I want to feel like the Queen.
I know what it takes to get the perfect picture and
that's not what I am going for.
I'm going for deep pleasure,
the kind that lives within me.
I'm going for Fierce Grace, and that, my friends, is
not for sale. This life is mine and I will live it
my way.

Live your one life
with your heart and your soul.

Light the fire.

Waxing Moon Phase: November 16-29. Full Moon November 30.

More than ever, we must sing hallelujah. We must rise up.

By calling on and giving to our communities, by using our Sadhana practice, and by standing in love, we can move through these times with grace.

We are being called upon to be soft yet fierce; we are being asked to hold innocence but not naïveté; we are being asked to be Strong Women. More than ever, we must rise to these challenges. We must flow like water and be accepting, but we must have clear boundaries and know where the river bank lies.

Your meditation practice will help you to fortify your being and prepare for a new year. Discipline comes in many forms, and every day we are given opportunities to practice what we want to be and how we want to live.

"I am a full-of-fire woman. I love
to rise early in the morning and
my days are filled with much that
I hold sacred."

—Carrie-Anne Moss

Bonus: Intentions

My intentions start with simplicity. The simple truth of what it is I'm really craving right now. I'm craving joy and laughter, I'm craving lightness and depth. I'm craving community and connection, I'm craving authentic conversations and I'm craving true listening, myself as the listener and also in being heard. I want to be able to be with my children and my husband in new and expansive ways, in order to know who they are. I want to be kind and patient and I want to make really delicious food. I want to be of service. I want to expand my heart and consciousness so that I understand how much I truly have to share and receive and to give. I want to listen to music 24 hours a day, even in my sleep. I want mantra! I want early morning Sadhana. Did I already say I want community? I want community, community, community. Simple and sincere community.

What are yours?

My intentions:

Journal

Journal

Waning Moon Phase: December 1-13. New Moon December 14.

To create spaciousness in this day and age takes effort.
And you know what? It's worth it. Spaciousness is our
sweet beloved friend who restores us, who brings peace
to our spirits and hearts and puts delight on the faces
of our lovers and our children. Life can be stressful
and people forget to create space. I encourage you to
embrace spaciousness as a radical act right now.
Prioritize it. Let it be part of your ritual, your
tradition. Let it be known that you value it.

What nourishes you? Can you look at yourself in the eye
and tell yourself that you are loved? Can you wrap
yourself in soft blankets and turn off your phone? Can
you make a simmering broth and feed it to yourself each
day?

Bonus: Letter to Winter

Dear Winter,

I want to hear your voice. I want to understand and take the time to hear your message to my heart. I want to nourish myself in every moment through what I think and how I interact with my beloveds. As I light the fire in the morning I will make a wish into the fire. Today it will be for laughter. And when I light it at dinner, as I bring the wood in from outside I will connect with reverence like I am a woman who lived deep in the forest years ago and who needed this fire to keep warm to thrive.

I will respect you that much.

I will drink ginger tea with homemade almond milk as I sit next to you, my dear strong friend.

I will write a poem for you today and I will take a bath as if it were the sweetest thing I could ever do.

I will do this because this most precious life of mine is a gift and I want to celebrate the mundane with all the magic I can.

Love,
Carrie-Anne

Dear Winter:

Journal

Journal

I AM

I Am

New Moon in Sagittarius
December 14

Full Moon in Cancer
December 30

Gesture to live in:
I am who I am.

Question:
What will I take with me?

Keywords:
Self
Knowing
Simplicity
Let go

*

Lunar New Year:
New Moon in Aquarius
January 24

I Am

I am who I am thank god I am.
I think this so many times a day.
I am grateful.
I am so grateful.

I have many tools that I lean on while navigating
these days, these months, these years.
I am who I am.
I am worthy.
I am true.
I am strong,
and clear and grounded.

When I am grounded and strong and connected
I can do anything.
Grounded women cannot be manipulated.

I will never be perfect (thank god).
Perfection kept me small and afraid.
I will live my life following the sound of me.
The gift of this life is to be true.

May we collectively rise with hearts wide open
To be all that we gloriously are.

I am the light of my soul
I am beautiful
I am bountiful
I am bliss

I am, I am.

Waxing Moon Phase: December 15-29. Full Moon December 30

When I bring things to my life, I want them to stretch me, but not complicate my life. Sure, there are many incredible meditations, but a simple practice feeds me and doesn't take from me. It's a fine line where to stretch and where to say, "This is good enough."

As we move through life navigating all the bits and pieces of our unique and personal experiences, there is always opportunity to grow. Our lives are our classroom. There will be days of ease and days of struggle and days of everything in between. With clarity, softness, strength and grit, we can ride the waves of our lives with grace and joy. Gone are the days of wishing things were different. Certainty starts within the depth of our soul.

"Can we really look at ourselves in the eye and tell ourselves that we are loved? Can we wrap ourselves in soft blankets and turn off our ringers? Can we make a simmering broth and feed it to ourselves each day? The answer is YES."

—Carrie-Anne Moss

Journal

Journal

Waning Moon Phase: December 31-January 12. New Moon January 12.

The end is truly the beginning. They are separated only by a hair. I invite you to look at the year ahead of you. When you close your eyes, picture yourself on the luminous precipice where past becomes future: the present.

Reflection is a keyword for you right now. Look how far you've come! How did you grow last year? What did you learn? What will you leave behind, what burdens have you learned to let go? As we move through life and become older, I like to think that we journey ever-closer to the center of our selves. We listen more to the whispers, we care less about what people think and we break the shackles of expectation, beauty norms and obligation. We find freedom in the simple and the mundane.

If you take a moment to look ahead and to dance in the possibility of creation and dreams, what do you see? What lies ahead for you? Potent themes for this season are home and security. Lift these up and away from obligation and bathe them in light and love. What remains?

Journal

Journal

Journal

Journal

credits + love:

Created by Carrie-Anne Moss
Design, edit, and layout by Sadie Rose Casey

Clip art graphics by Lille Studio
Annapurna Living painting (p.5) by Rachael Rice
Watercolor washes by Digital Press Creations
Drawings (p. 18, 19, 173) by Janae Macy
Moon Chart (p. 16) by Loretta Neal

www.annapurnaliving.com
www.fiercegracecollective.com

CPSIA information can be obtained
at www.ICGtesting.com
Printed in the USA
LVHW070916261119
638364LV00004BA/13/P

9 780464 425304